Finding the Answers in the Individual Deceased Personnel File

Written by Jennifer Holik

WWII Research and Writing Center Publishing

Editors: Sarah Ferguson Potter and Johan van Waart
Cover Designer: Jennifer Holik

Holik, Jennifer, 1973 –
        Finding the Answers in the Individual Deceased Personnel
File / Jennifer Holik. Includes bibliographical references and index-
es.

ISBN: 978-1-938226-43-4
ISBN: 1-938226-43-7

Also By Jennifer Holik

Finding the Answers: Researching World War II Army Service Part 1

Finding the Answers: Researching World War II Army Service Part 2

Finding the Answers: Researching Women in World War II

Finding the Answers: World War II Travel in Europe

Finding the Answers in the Individual Deceased Personnel File

Finding the Answers: Discovering World War II Service Online

Faces of War Researching Your Adopted Soldier

Stories from the World War II Battlefield
World War II Writing Prompts

Stories from the World War II Battlefield Volume 3
Writing the Stories of War

Stories from the World War II Battlefield Volume 2
Navigating the Service Records for the Navy, Coast Guard, Marine Corps, and Merchant Marines

Stories from the World War II Battlefield Volume 1
Reconstructing Army, Air Corps, and National Guard Service

Stories from the Battlefield:
A Beginning Guide to World War II Research

The Tiger's Widow

Stories of the Lost

Engaging the Next Generation:

A Guide for Genealogy Societies and Libraries

Branching Out: Genealogy for Adults

Branching Out: Genealogy for High School Students

Branching Out: Genealogy for 4th-8th Grades Students

Branching Out: Genealogy for 1st-3rd Grade Students

To Soar with the Tigers

Dedication

For all those preserving the stories of our WWII service members.

Acknowledgements

I could not have written this book without the support of my husband Johan and my three amazing boys, Andrew, Luke, and Tyler. Thank you for always believing in me and listening to me talk through research problems. I love you all.

Virginia Davis for her constant love, encouragement, and support as I wrote all my World War II books.

Over the last five years, many amazing and knowledgeable researchers have contributed to the knowledge I have today. They include, Thulai van Maanen, Norm Richards, Jonathan Webb Deiss, Mike Constandy, Sarah Ferguson Potter, Mary Hoyer, Connie Yen, Lisa Alzo, Eric Bijtelaar, Doug Mitchell, Tom Scholtes, Vincent Orrière, Ryan Kelly, Mikel Shilling, Herman Wolters, and Sebastiaan Vonk.

A big thank you to all my clients. Through every project I expanded my knowledge which allows me to share more with others. Thank you to everyone who attended my military lectures and told me their stories or asked questions. I cannot forget the individuals who emailed me or chatted with me on social media about their soldier's story. I learned something from each of those encounters which helped create my programs and books.

Table of Contents

Introduction

During World War II, over 400,000 Americans died and currently, 73,000 are still considered Missing In Action (MIA). Of those 73,000, some are buried as Unknowns in American Battle Monument Commission (ABMC) cemeteries. The remaining were buried at sea or have never been recovered.

It has only been in the last three to five years, that the public has become more aware that a file was created for each service member, a few civilians who died during military service, and also a few children. This file is the Individual Deceased Personnel File (IDPF). Six plus years ago, primarily those searching for MIAs or more serious military historians knew of the IDPF's existence. In the last four to five years, family historians, grave adopters, and other researchers have learned of its existence and started requesting the file. During this time period, the IDPF was almost impossible to get in a reasonable amount of time due to custody and handling of the files. Now however, these files for surnames A-L are in the custody of the National Personnel Records Center (NPRC) and can be accessed and received within a few months rather than several years. Surnames M-Z are supposed to be available at NPRC at some point in 2018.

For those reading this book who are researching someone who died in World War I, there is a similar file called the Burial File, in the custody of the National Personnel Records Center (NPRC) in St. Louis, Missouri. Further, regardless of military branch, the files for both World Wars, contain similar documents and the same process was used by the Graves Registration Service teams that handled the remains.

This IDPF is required for anyone researching the World War II service of those who died or are still MIA. It is as important at the Official Military Personnel File (OMPF). There is a myth circulating that the IDPF contains all the information from the OMPF. This file does not serve as a replacement if the OMPF burned in the 1973 fire, though it may contain a brief summary of training dates and locations.

The IDPF documents the death, identification, temporary and permanent burial of our war dead. Search and recovery history is usually included in files for remains located in isolated burial sites. Photographs of the individual from induction in the military are often found in Navy, Coast Guard, Marine Corps, and Merchant Marine IDPFs. Additionally, the files often contain handwritten letters from the family members to the military and U.S. government asking questions or responding to correspondence.

For the unidentified who are buried as Unknowns in our ABMC cemeteries, there is a X-File. The X-File identifies remains with a number known as the X number because no Service Number is known. The IDPF identifies remains by the individual's Serial Number/Service Number. The X-File contains all paperwork related to the unknown set of remains or multiple remains buried together including additional forensic data and lists of others who are still MIA. The file contents are basically the same as an IDPF with slightly more information that might contain clues to identify remains.

Many questions surround these files and the deaths of those for whom these files were created. Who created these files? What do researchers need to know about the contents of these files? Why are they so important? Where were our service members buried? What happened to the remains that were identified or not identified? Why did some families choose to leave their service member buried overseas? What did the government tell the families when they were notified about the death? What did they not tell the families? What happened to the cemeteries in which our honored dead rest? What family history information and family dynamics do we see in these files? What family secrets and turmoil are uncovered?

We will **Find the Answers** to these questions in this volume.

Locating Details of Service and Death

There is a strategy to military research. A strategy that is unique in the educational materials provided by the World War II Research and Writing Center. This book will not be a comprehensive focus on the research strategy. The focus will center around locating details about the death, recovery, burial, or MIA status of our service members.

Researching your service member's history can be complex. The World War II Research and Writing Center provides research experts to tackle your most challenging research questions. Contact us at info@wwiirwc.com for project details and costs. We have researchers on-site at the National Archives facilities to obtain materials within a few weeks, and a network of researchers and tour guides around the globe.

Service History

Through a two-part research strategy we can identify the service history of an individual. We can learn about his enlistment and discharge or death. Where he trained and the dates of each training. Family information and medical information. When he was transferred overseas and returned. Campaigns or battles in which he participated. Details about his death or MIA status.

Death Details

One of the first things to be aware of when looking at death information, is that this is only one piece of the entire puzzle. The unit information that is on a Report of Burial or listed in the IDPF, is only the final unit. In many cases, it was not the only unit in which someone served.

One should never assume the one piece of information you have is the whole story. It is a stepping stone to move forward or backward through the military records to learn more.

For example, my cousin James Privoznik was Killed In Action 11 January 1945 during the Battle of the Bulge. His grave shows the 358th Infantry Regiment 90th Infantry Division. Had I researched the 358th Infantry Regiment's history for the entire time they were overseas, I would have only learned a fraction of James' service history.

James was a rifleman in that infantry regiment for only 14 days before he was killed. Patton needed replacement soldiers for the front lines during the Battle of the Bulge and men were taken from rear echelons and put on the front lines. Using this infantry regiment as a starting point I was able to reconstruct James' service moving backward and discovered he was part of the 790th Ordnance Medium Maintenance Company the rest of the nine months he was overseas with the 90th Infantry Division. He had two completely different war experiences.

Where else can we find death details? This information is also captured in Company Morning Reports (Army and Army Air Forces) and Crew Lists and Muster Rolls (Navy, Marines, Coast Guard, and Merchant Marines.) The reports mentioned are daily or monthly reports in which any change to a service member's status within the organization was recorded. Associated records, like the Missing Air Crew Report (MACR), Mission Reports, and Accident Reports provide additional details. The death may have been mentioned in numerous other records. These are a few examples of the most common places to find answers to your questions.

Asking Questions

When a service member was listed as MIA or confirmed dead, a telegram was sent to the legal next-of-kin. If the service member was married, this was his wife or widow. If he was not, the hierarchy of legal next-of-kin was father, mother, (or legal guardian), then down the line of siblings.

Sometimes a letter would follow from a Chaplain or another military agent whose job it was to console the families, and provide vague details about the missing status or death. The families might hear nothing for several years until the war ended, unless in rare cases, they pushed for answers. It wasn't until 1946 that families were notified of the temporary burial location of their service member who had been confirmed dead. If that soldier had died in 1942 in North Africa or the Pacific, four years is a long time to wait for information. Even families who received notification of those who died after D-Day in 1944, had to wait until 1946.

The lack of information to the public about policies and procedures for our honored dead combined with the sparse letters sent from the government to the families, left people with many questions and often additional pain. Unfortunately, most of the families never received answers to their questions while they lived. It is their descendants, the children and grandchildren, who now have access to the IDPF and who are now obtaining answers. Yet there are cases where the information only begs for more questions to which we may never have answers.

Why was there such a lack of communication? The 1940s was a time in which telephones did not exist in every home. People communicated by letter, postcard, telegram, and word of mouth. Looking through the historical lens we must remember there were no smart phones or social media, which most of us are accustomed to today, and some cannot remember a time in their life when that wasn't in existence.

It was an enormous undertaking to keep track of all the men and women who served, through paper records, and transmit that information home. Form letters were created to make the information transfer easier, which provided the bare minimum in answers. It seems only educated, wealthy, socially connected men who demanded answers, received them. Anyone who did not fall into this category received the usual form letters and not much else in the way of answers.

Over the last five years, I've spent thousands of hours reading ID-PFs for all service branches. I've explored further into the lives and deaths of many of these individuals. Many of the same questions rise from the family members through communication with the government or military, and within me as I read new files. What are some of these questions?

General Questions

Who created these files? Do I need to explore the history of the Graves Registration Unit who recovered my soldier?

When were families notified about the MIA status or confirmed death?

What did the government tell (or not tell) the families through official correspondence when they were notified about the death?

What happened to the remains that were identified or not identified?

What did the government pay for as part of final burial?

Why did some families choose to leave their service member buried overseas? Was money ever an issue?

Family Questions

What are the death details? When, where, how, did he suffer?

Where is he buried?

He died as a POW. When can I have his body back?

What happened to the personal effects? Why are some missing?

Who receives his death benefits and insurance?

Who determines where the remains are to be permanently interred?

What happens if the widow of the serviceman remarried after his death and prior to the final decisions?

What personal effects were recovered and sent home? For example, why did one soldier have a $200,000 personal check in his personal effects overseas?

What happens if he is never recovered and remains in MIA status?

What happened to the cemeteries in which our honored dead rest?

What family history information and family dynamics do we see in these files?

What family secrets and drama are uncovered?

General Biographical and Service History Questions

The following questions are often asked by family members researching their service member, but also European grave adopters who honor the memory of our American service members. European grave adopters generally want to know the basics of the individual's death and to locate family, and a photograph. On the other side of that coin, there are some grave adopters who want to know the individual's entire service history, locate family, and photographs. These are some questions which are asked.

When was service member born?

When did he enlist, or what was the induction date?

What was his service number?

Where did he train?

If applicable, when did he become an officer?

What unit(s) was he in?

Who was his next-of-kin? Is there any evidence of a remarriage of the widow?

Is there information about other relatives in service?

When was he KIA, declared MIA or POW, or had a FOD? What were the circumstances surrounding his death and recovery?

When and where was he buried?

Finding Answers

These are only a few questions that rise in the course of research. To begin finding the answers, let's begin with exploring the history of the American Graves Registration Service (AGRS), who created the IDPF documents.

American Graves Registration Service

Upon conclusion of both World Wars, the U.S. government began bringing home the soldiers who survived and handling the final disposition of those who did not. Due to high numbers of Soldier Dead buried overseas, the government established permanent American Military Cemeteries overseas. Families had the choice to permanently bury their soldier who was killed overseas in an American Military Cemetery or have the soldier's remains repatriated and buried in a cemetery in the United States.

After World War II, for the families who chose to leave the remains of their service member overseas, and for the unknown soldiers, re-interment in permanent American Military Cemeteries took place after all the repatriated dead were returned home. The 209 temporary cemeteries across Europe, North Africa, and the Pacific were condensed to 14 cemeteries in foreign countries.[1]

****

Soldier Dead is a term used by the military to describe those valiant men and women who gave the ultimate sacrifice during military service. This term will be used throughout this chapter to refer to our honored war dead.

****

Today, the American Battle Monuments Commission (ABMC) oversees the cemeteries which hold our American military dead around the world. ABMC was established in 1923 by Congress to honor our Great War dead.[2] These cemeteries were granted in perpetuity to our government and remain tax free. Burial in these cemeteries was not just of our male G.I.'s but also, women service members, civilians, war correspondents, children, Red Cross workers, USO entertainers, and other military personnel during World War I and II.

The cemeteries were laid out to be green, expansive, beautiful, and full of peace. Each headstone is made of marble in the shape of a cross or Star of David, depending on the religion of the soldier. Visitor's centers were erected in some cemeteries, which depict the history of battles fought nearby. In each cemetery there is a Wall or Tablet of the Missing which lists the names of the missing. Those who have been identified since these Walls were erected, now have a Rosette placed next to their name, showing they were finally identified and no longer carry the Missing In Action status.

The cemeteries are groomed and cared for by AMBC staff. Europeans often decorate the graves with flags and flowers for commemorative ceremonies throughout the year. The ABMC offers photography services for families who wish to have a photograph of their service member's grave and the cemetery. Some cemeteries offer floral services if you wish to have flowers placed on a soldier's grave, or can recommend a local florist. All ABMC cemeteries have Memorial Day commemorative services. During the days preceding these services, many people come from around the world to lay flowers at the graves and honor the service member buried there. The commemoration service often includes speeches by ABMC staff, Military Personnel, and dignitaries. The service also contains music, wreath laying by organizations, an honor guard, prayers, and often a military fly-over at the conclusion.

To fully appreciate how these cemeteries came into existence and honor those buried beneath the foreign soil, we must discuss the men who helped build the cemeteries. Who were they? What kind of job did they have during and after the wars? How did they care for our most honored dead? And how did they shape the cemeteries we visit today?

These men were from the Quartermaster Graves Registration Service. What follows is not an exhaustive history of this unit because many books have been written on the subject. The purpose is to provide an overview to help put each soldier's life and death into greater context.

American Graves Registration Service History

The American Graves Registration Service (AGRS) has a long history dating back to 1862 when Congress gave the President authorization to create permanent American military cemeteries. This act gave the President the ability to seek and purchase land for these cemeteries.[3] In 1867 Congress gave the Quartermaster General in the U.S. Army the responsibility to establish military cemeteries, handle burials, keep records, and handle ongoing maintenance of these cemeteries.[4] The Quartermaster handled the burials of our soldiers from the Civil War, Spanish-American War and World War I.

During World War I, the number of dead was approximately 77,000, scattered over many battlefields. They were temporarily buried in 2,400 cemeteries in England and Europe.[5] Eventually roughly ¾ of these Soldier Dead were either repatriated to the U.S. or interred in one of the eight permanent military cemeteries in England or Europe. When World War I ended, the AGRS worked to consolidate these cemeteries and recover remains buried in enemy lands.

When the U.S. entered World War II, one thing the Army decided, was to not establish thousands of small cemeteries. Instead, they planned to establish larger cemeteries near the fighting and bring the dead to these cemeteries. Collection points were established so the combat units could assist in the collection and identification of the deceased. The AGRS men found if identification could take place near the battlefield with information from the combat unit there was a higher chance of positively identifying the deceased. When the unit had moved on and no one was available to help identify the dead, many were brought to the collection points and cemeteries as Unknowns.

The Job

When we think of a cemetery in the U.S. or one of the ABMC cemeteries, we picture a beautiful, expansive, quiet, peaceful, rolling green, lush, and clean cemetery. Just as we are conditioned to think of our World War II veterans as older men and women, we are conditioned to see military cemeteries as beautiful. This was not always the case.

As the U.S. prepared for war, the men of the AGRS were trained to go with the troops and handle the casualties. AGRS workers were responsible for locating suitable cemetery sites overseas. Once selected after examining the terrain, soil quality, and distance to enemy lines, they began plotting the cemetery. Maps were drawn, processing tents were set up and the men assigned tasks. Local civilian workers were called in to help dig graves and bury the dead.

The job of an AGRS man was not glamorous. Nor was it discussed and publicized very often. As unsung heroes, these men worked tirelessly to care for the remains of not only our U.S. dead, Allied dead, but also enemy dead. Within practically every U.S. temporary cemetery, there was a section for German dead. AGRS men worked to identify every casualty they buried. This was not always possible. When information was gathered and documented about the unidentified soldiers, duplicates of some of those documents were placed in a canister and buried in the grave.

Why were both Allied and enemy dead buried in these temporary cemeteries? It was important to bury all the dead primarily for health reasons. Decomposing bodies out in the open would spread disease and lower troop morale. It was better the troops, when possible, did not encounter the remains of their comrades, lest the fear and panic they already felt increase.

There was also the respect for the fallen and families back home. Our men and women made the ultimate sacrifice for their country. They deserved respect from those who cared for them after death since their families could not.

The dead were buried for forensic reasons. Information was gathered to not only identify them but also explain how they were killed. Furthermore, AGRS buried for political reasons which showed both allies and enemies we have a heart, are human, and care for others with compassion.

The AGRS in World War II was not only responsible for collecting, identifying, and burying the dead, but also handling personal effects. The men had a system by which they worked to gather, inventory, and bag remaining personal effects. The effects were sent to an Effects Depot in the U.S. where they would be re-inventoried, cleaned if necessary, and prepared for shipment to the family.

There were many people who made up the Quartermaster Graves Registration (QMGR) Unit. The individuals who primarily handled the dead are described here. The description which follows is not meant to be an exhaustive look at the make-up of the QMGR Unit, but to give a general idea of some components. An in-depth examination can be found in the *Department of the Army Field Manual 10-29* and *Department of the Army Field Manual 10-63*. AGRS personnel duties varied by person. Each was trained for a specific job during and after basic training.

AGRS Platoon Headquarters

Platoon Leader

The Platoon Leader's duties varied depending on whether or not the platoon was part of the company at the time of operation. Overall the Platoon Leader selected a cemetery site and was responsible for training, discipline, supplies, and transportation. When the platoon was part of the company, other miscellaneous duties were assigned.[6]

Platoon Sergeant

The Platoon Sergeant assisted the Platoon Leader in his duties.[7]

Surveyor

The Surveyor supervised the layout of the cemeteries. He usually trained a team to work with him to clear a space for use.[8]

Other Positions

The Liaison Agent served as a replacement for the Platoon Leader at various meetings. A Supply Specialist requisitioned and maintained stock for the unit. And a Light Truck Driver was the messenger for the Platoon and had miscellaneous duties as assigned.[9]

AGRS Collection and Evacuation Section

Section Chief

The Section Chief was the supervisor of all the AGRS specialists. In certain situations when the combat troops are unable to help evacuate the Soldier Dead, the Section Chief assumes this responsibility.[10]

Graves Registration Specialists

Graves Registration Specialists were specifically trained in receiving Soldier Dead, identification procedures, record keeping, effects collection and distribution, and burial. These men worked with Assistant Graves Registration Specialists who had many of the same tasks.[11]

Graves Registration Clerk

The duties of the Graves Registration Clerk were to prepare all the reports on the Soldier Dead which became part of the Individual Deceased Personnel File (IDPF) and were sent to Headquarters in weekly reports.[12]

Still Photographer

A Still Photographer was used in cases where remains could not be identified. The photographer took photographs of the face and torso, tattoos, other identifying markings on the body and fingers in case prints could be identified.[13]

Technical Operations Personnel

Graves Registration Chief

The Graves Registration Chief supervised the Technical Operations Personnel under his command. He also oversaw four platoons and planned personnel jobs and in some cases, the cemeteries.[14]

Identification Chief

The Identification Chief worked with the Graves Registration Chief to supervise all the teams who worked with the Soldier Dead. He ensured the effects were transferred appropriately, records were completed, and as often as possible, each soldier was identified. He was also responsible for, "taking of fingerprints, preparation of tooth charts, …..and recording of accurate physical descriptions on appropriate forms."[15]

Draftsman

The Draftsman planned the cemetery layout and plotted it on a map.[16]

Fluoroscope Operator

The Fluoroscope Operator had an important job within the Technical Operations Personnel group. He was responsible for scanning the body using x-ray, to identify the location of identification tags which may have become embedded in the body. He also looked for possible foreign bodies such as shrapnel, unexploded devices, and other objects. When needed, the Fluoroscope Operator ran a chemical laboratory.[17]

Carpenter

The Carpenter handled all the usual carpentry duties within a AGRS unit including creating crosses for the grave markers, building fences around the cemeteries, constructing signs to direct Collection Units and others to the AGRS collecting points or cemeteries, and other miscellaneous duties as required.18

Obstacles for the Graves Registration Service

Pacific Theater of War

AGRS were not always present at battles in the Pacific Theater of War therefore, the burial of the dead was left primarily to the Marines and Navy units on the islands of battle. Temporary cemeteries were established, often using the trench burial system, to bury soldiers. A trench burial system was basically a long ditch, rather than individually dug graves, in which several remains would be buried. The burial party would erect some sort of marker or cross over each set of remains before departing. The temporary cemeteries established were not always plotted, charted, or properly documented as to who was buried in them, as was done in the European Theater. This led to major identification and recovery issues after the war.

Record keeping was sparse, and for many of the soldiers killed, you will not find complete IDPFs with Reports of Burial like you might in the European Theater. Notations may have been made in a personnel file or the file contains telegrams or letters sent to the family of the deceased.

A primary example of the lack of records is the Battle of Tarawa in the Gilbert Islands in November 1943. In the Battle of Tarawa, many Marines lost their lives. The dead had to be buried quickly because the small island was covered in thousands of American and Japanese war dead. The threat of disease was high and we needed to ensure our troops were properly buried. Trench burial was the primary burial method used to quickly bury the dead. Families were notified, based on limited information, that their Marine had died and was buried on Tarawa.

After hostilities ceased on the island, the Navy Seabees came in to take care of the cemeteries. Not being trained in AGRS procedures, many of the remains were disinterred without proper documentation. Also, in an attempt to clean up the cemeteries, grave markers were moved, but the remains were not. This led to great confusion as to who was actually buried in a certain grave, when the war ended. Families later received a letter stating the remains of their Marine could not be located or repatriated. Today, efforts are ongoing by many organizations to identify and repatriate these valiant men.

European Theater of War

As well-prepared and trained as AGRS men were, nothing could have prepared them for the onslaught of dead, which would appear when the Allies invaded the beaches of Normandy on June 6, 1944.

The AGRS men participating in the Normandy Invasion were underprepared for the number of soldiers who would be killed during the invasion. Improvising along the way, these AGRS men established ways to track both the identification of Soldier Dead and their belongings. It was not, however, a perfect system. Not only were the dead brought to each collecting station, but the AGRS men were given maps and coordinates of temporary graves or downed planes and gliders which needed to be cleared.

Colonel Elbert E. Legg, a AGRS Sergeant in the 603rd Quartermaster Graves Registration Company, stated they used parachutes as a burial shroud since they had landed without mattress covers.[19] The number of dead arriving daily, even before the cemetery could be marked out, exceeded their supplies and manpower. Until more manpower was brought in, the bare minimum was done in tracking personal effects. At one point, Colonel Legg was required to move to a new sector due to heavy enemy fighting. He tied up the personal effects bags in a parachute and hid it in a hedgerow until he could return to the area.[20]

We must always keep in mind, especially when discussing any facet of war, the fact that the men did the best they could at the time with the resources and knowledge they had. It was war. War is hell, full of chaos and confusion. Bullets flew as battled raged, which made it difficult for the AGRS men to do their jobs perfectly when they received each new dead soldier. Record keeping was done primarily by paper and pencil in the combat zone. Computer record keeping did not exist. DNA did not exist. It was a much different time, one which we need to remember when we begin to judge why more men were not identified. We have to view this job through the historical lens.

Establishing Temporary Cemeteries

Before a cemetery could be established and Soldier Dead collected and buried, sites had to be examined. AGRS men looked for good terrain, sites close to main roads, and with natural protection in the form of trees or hedges. These trees or hedges would grow over time and offer more privacy to the cemetery grounds. They also checked soil conditions, evaluated drainage, looked for potential mines, and the destruction which surrounded the potential cemetery area. In some cases, AGRS men looked for areas near combat zones where they knew heavy fighting would occur. This made it somewhat easier to transport and collect the Soldier Dead.

When a cemetery was laid out, there were certain guidelines to be followed.[21] These included:

- Graves were to be at least five feet in depth.

- When soldiers were interred, the head of each should face the same direction.

- A marker was to be placed at the head of each grave.

- Graves were to be numbered consecutively.

- If a trench burial system had to be implemented, the same procedure for laying out Soldier Dead was followed.

- Graves should align horizontally and vertically with other graves.

- A cemetery map should be drawn for indicating north. Separate plans should be drawn for each cemetery or burial plot if it is a trench burial. A trench burial system of burial meant a backhoe or similar machine dug a long ditch in which bodies would be buried.

A bivouac site, or camping area, was selected near the cemetery site which provided shelter from the weather, water, good drainage, and was free of disease. When possible, AGRS men selected towns which provided undamaged homes, hospitals, schools, and other buildings to house the men.

In some cases, the dead would not be buried in temporary cemeteries, but in temporary graves on the battlefield. Combat units were instructed to create a burial duty of at least two soldiers to bury the dead as quickly as possible. Due to combat conditions, there was not enough time to fill out paperwork or pull identification tags or personal effects. The dead were buried and some marker was placed at their grave and notes written to indicate where the remains were located. The AGRS men would later sweep the battlefields and disinter these hastily buried men.[22]

The Collection Point - Remains Recovery Process

A Collection Point was established on a main road and was used as the location to which the Soldier Dead were brought, usually by units in combat or AGRS men. Collection Points contained an administrative tent, examination tent, examination area, and a screen to shelter passing troops from the view of their dead comrades.

The AGRS men at Collection Points identified when possible, collected personal effects, and transported the remains to the nearest American cemetery for burial. When they arrived at a cemetery, AGRS workers again checked identification, effects, and rechecked records before temporary burial occurred.

AGRS claimed the remains of a soldier from a unit, along the road side or battle ground. Men worked in the mud, rain, deep snow, jungles and on beaches in their recovery efforts. During December and January 1945, when the Battle of the Bulge raged, the weather was bitter cold and snow packed the ground for weeks. This made the job of grave digging and handling the dead ever more difficult.[23] These men also crossed back and forth over enemy lines putting their own lives in danger.

The recovery process was meant to collect both complete bodies and scattered remains. Consider the soldier who received a gunshot wound to the head. That most likely constituted a complete body or set of remains. Now, think about the men hit by shells. These bodies would have been in all sorts of condition, and may have been scattered around the area in which they were killed. AGRS could not always attend to the dead immediately after they were killed, so these men encountered all stages of decomposition.

What Soldiers Carried

A common question families asked when they received word their service member was dead was, "Where are his personal effects?" Families wanted every piece of their soldier they could get, both as a way to remember them and to grieve for them.

It is important to note that all usable clothing, shoes and equipment were stripped off and sent to the Quartermaster Supply Depots to be reused. What families were not told is that the soldiers carried very little of what was theirs on their person. The Army issued their clothing, bags, and equipment. They did wear identification tags, and may have carried Bibles, diaries, wallets, rings, insignia, letters, photos, and money; but little else was theirs.

What happened to the things they carried? The enemy may have picked items off the dead. The soldier may have sold or given away watches and such. Friends may have taken an item off their dead buddy for safekeeping. Or it may have been destroyed when the soldier was killed.[24] There were other reasons personal effects may have been missing. Duffle bags were usually on a truck or ship, and not always near the troops. In cases where the truck or ship was bombed or hit a mine and blew up, the personal effects were likely lost.

Effects collected were bagged and sent to the Effects Bureau in Kansas City, Missouri. Here, effects were cleaned of blood and grime. It was then determined if the effect should be returned to the family. In some cases, things were not sent to the family.

For instance, if letters from a girlfriend were found on a soldier, and he was married, based on the service records, those letters would have been destroyed. If an item was destroyed or badly damaged as a result of the cause of death, those items were described to the family in a letter. The family was then given the choice as to whether or not they wanted the item.

Most families were happy to receive anything from their soldier, and sent letters to the Quartermaster thanking them for sending the effects. I have read IDPFs in which the family felt their grief was too much to bear and told the government they did not wish to have any personal effects, did not wish for the remains to be brought home, and chose to have no further communication with the government or military. Each family dealt with their loss in their own way. There were cases where the Quartermaster received letters from family members accusing them of being thieves and the lowest men on earth for "stealing" money or other items from their Soldier Dead.

The government did not educate the public about the chaos overseas or the work of the AGRS men and the conditions under which they worked. Combine this with the pain and grief of a family member, and anger and hate was directed at the only place they could think of, the Quartermaster General in the Effects Bureau.

Identification Process

When a service member's remains, either U.S. or enemy, were recovered, every attempt at identification took place. The procedure for processing remains and identification began at the stripping line, where troops initially removed explosives and equipment. Another soldier would take these items to a nearby ammo and equipment area so they could be inventoried and reissued.

The next step was when medical sergeants came in with a clerk. The sergeants cut pockets and other pieces of clothing in order to locate identification tags and remove personal effects. Typically, these men worked without gloves in destroyed and decomposed remains. Identification tags were sought as part of this process, even when the remains were in bad condition.

To identify remains, identification tags were sought first. If those could not be recovered, then a soldier's comrades were consulted, if they were available, to help identify the soldier. Rings, insignia, pay records, letters and photographs that may have been carried were also used in the process. In some cases, dental records and laundry marks were used.

Upon first issue of clothing in the Army, a soldier would put a laundry mark in his clothing to show that it was his. This mark was the first letter of his surname plus the last four digits of his serial number. However, when serving on the front lines, when a soldier entered a wash-up station, he may or may not have had his duffle bag with his clothing available. In those cases, the men stripped, left their clothing, went into the wash station on one end, came out the other and were given new clothes. It was the hope that the clothes were the size they needed, but this was not always the case. Because clothes were reissued over and over, there may have been several different laundry marks, which would have made it very difficult to positively identify the remains.

Positive Identification

When a Soldier Dead was identified, a mattress cover which, was used as a shroud, was prepared for him by painting his name, rank, and serial number on it. Then his remains were arranged and closed in the shroud. One identification tag was inserted into deceased's mouth, or somewhere else on his remains, before he was placed in a grave. The other identification tag was attached to the cross on the grave. Next, paperwork would be sent to the War Department in order to notify the next of kin. The bags of personal effects were shipped to Kansas City, MO.

Unknown Identification

Not all Soldier Dead were identified because of the condition of the body when it was received by the AGRS. Other factors included advanced decomposition, as well as none of the soldier's comrades being available to help identify him.

To assist in identification, a still photographer was brought in to photograph the face, torso and other identifying marks on the body when the remains were in a condition this would be helpful. Photos were also taken of the fingers and hands in case prints could not be obtained. A fluoroscope was used to see if the identification tags were embedded in the body or if other foreign matter resided there.

When all available identification options were exhausted and remains could not be identified, they were assigned an X number since there was no serial number by which to identify them. This X number was placed on reports. Duplicate reports were created for the unknown soldiers. When possible, fingerprints of all 10 fingers were taken and put into the Report of Death.[25] Unknown remains were placed into a mattress cover and X number was painted on the bag. The personal effects were shipped to Kansas City, MO.

Two metallic tags with the X number were made. One was inserted into deceased's mouth and the other was attached to the cross on the grave. The duplicate copy of records was placed in a bottle and buried with Soldier Dead. This allowed for possible identification at a later time when the remains were disinterred.

In cases where bodies were mangled or adhered together due to a plane crash or other disaster, if the AGRS men were unable to disentangle the remains, a group burial would have been conducted. In these cases most were unidentified because the remains were destroyed beyond recognition.[26]

The Individual Deceased Personnel File (IDPF)

This section is comprised of two parts. First, I will explain the common contents of an IDPF. Second, I will explain how the IDPF can be used to start research and reconstruct details of a burned personnel file.

One of the <u>most</u> important things you can do to ease the analysis of an IDPF is to print it and put the documents in date order. Alternatively, as most files are digitized as PDFs, you can rearrange pages within a PDF. The records are never in date order, which can make analysis even more confusing. Print the file, no matter how lengthy, and place it in date order.

When a soldier was declared Missing in Action (MIA) or Killed in Action (KIA), an IDPF was created. Why was a death file created when a soldier was declared missing? It was rare someone who was declared missing ever returned alive, unless they were declared a Prisoner of War (POW). The file would be started, and it would include a Battle Casualty Report that listed the soldier as MIA. If the soldier was recovered later, his status would be changed to KIA. If he was never recovered, he would receive a Finding of Death (FOD) and his death date would be at least one year plus one day after his MIA status began.

The IDPF was created for service members who could be identified, and each record contained at least the soldier's name and service number. If the remains were brought to the AGRS or a cemetery, and could not be identified, a file with the same contents as the IDPF was created, but it was called an X-File.

The X-File used an X-number in place of a service number. The X-number was assigned based on the next burial of an unknown soldier in a temporary cemetery. Each temporary cemetery had its own X-numbering system.

Details on the soldier would be recorded in the X-File just as it would have the IDPF. A match to a soldier would be attempted. In cases where an unknown soldier with an X-File was identified, the X-File was usually, but not always, merged into the IDPF. I've seen files where the identification could not possibly be accurate and the X-File paperwork was not merged. Researchers say the X-File papers were usually destroyed if remains were identified, but that was not always the case.

Statuses for Service Members

Statuses were assigned to service members when they were no longer present and accounted for within a unit. You will see these and other statuses in the IDPF, however the ones explained here are the most commonly seen.

Missing in Action (MIA). The MIA status was given to any soldier if he did not return to his unit within 24 hours of being listed on the previous day's report. For Army personnel, the change may not be shown on a report the following day, but several days later as information reached the clerk. An airman would likely show a status change the following day after a mission. Airmen were easier to track and report because they either returned from a mission or they did not.

Prisoner of War (POW). The POW status was given to a soldier declared MIA if word reached the military through the enemy or Red Cross.

Killed in Action (KIA). The KIA status was given to a soldier who was KIA and his body was recovered soon after the death, or his death was verified by at least one other soldier. What does this mean? An example of a verified death is one in which several men were seen getting in a boat to cross a river. Men from the shore witnessed the men crossing and drowning. Even if their remains were not recovered, they are given a KIA status because other soldiers confirmed their deaths. This is the official date of death. However, when no one can confirm the death, the MIA status went into effect until the remains were recovered or a Finding of Death was issued.

Finding of Death (FOD). The FOD status was given to a soldier when he had been MIA for a year plus one day if his remains had not been recovered. The FOD or Presumed Date of Death is the official date of death, even though it is likely the soldier died before the year plus one day. This was done according to the provisions of Section 5 of Public Law 490, 77th Congress, 7 March 1942.[27] When a soldier was officially declared deceased, the family could claim the insurance benefits, any pay due the soldier, and begin closing the estate.

The Marine Corps is one branch with an exception to this rule. Marines lost in enemy territory and declared MIA were removed from their unit's Muster Rolls and placed on a Detachment of Prisoners of War Muster Rolls for the year of MIA status. At the end of one year, the MIA cases were reviewed and a determination was made as to a FOD status or continued MIA status. The reason given for a continued MIA status was the possibility the Marine was a POW. It was not until the war in the Pacific ended, all the POW camps were evacuated, that those still considered MIA were given a FOD.

This was the case for USMC Pilot 1st Lt. Robert E. Bishop and his gunner, Pfc. Richard L. Parrow, who were declared MIA 17 January 1944. Their cases were reviewed in 1945, and a determination of continued MIA status was made.[28] The case was reviewed again in January 1946 after the cessation of hostilities with Japan. The military had emptied the POW camps in the Pacific and interviewed detainees. No information on Bishop or Parrow was discovered, and the men were given a FOD on 15 January 1946. Paperwork in Bishop's service file provided detailed documentation of the findings. A letter explaining the findings was sent to Bishop's parents.[29]

Unrecoverable Status. A status of Unrecoverable was given to a soldier in his IDPF, in most cases, if the remains could not be recovered due to the circumstances surrounding their death, the location of death, and they were lost and unable to be found. For example, many of the sailors and Marines aboard the USS Oklahoma were deemed unrecoverable after the ship sunk. According to the IDPF for Fireman 1st Class Samuel W. Crowder, a report by a Graves Registration Board stated the following regarding the recoverability of the personnel on that ship.

"Information in this headquarters indicates that the above-named personnel, consisting of eleven (11) marines, seven (7) Navy officers and there hundred fifty (350) Navy enlisted men, were aboard the USS OKLAHOMA when that vessel was sunk during the Japanese bombing raid on Pearl Harbor, Oahu, Territory of Hawaii on 7 December 1941. Available records also show that 25 persons were recovered and interred as known burials at the time of the incident and an additional (34) remains have been identified by the AGRS-PAZ Board of Review. No further information is available. (Exhibit B.)"[30]

In 2017, Samuel Crowder was finally identified by Defense Prisoners of War Missing Personnel (DPAA) and his remains were sent home for burial. He will have a Rosette placed next to his name on the Tablet of the Missing at the Punchbowl.

Another example of service members being unrecoverable due to location could be a bomb crew who crashed into the ocean. If the plane did not sink in shallow water, the likelihood of the remains being recovered was slim. Another example is a POW who died in a camp and was buried in the camp's cemetery. In Eastern Europe, the Soviet Army took over several POW camp grounds or towns, and turned them into a Soviet Army Training Bases or other installations. When the war ended, AGRS members were not allowed to recover the remains of possible U.S. servicemen buried there. There are many individuals buried in Eastern Europe who may never be recovered unless the political situation changes.

Contents of an IDPF

The main components of an IDPF are generally the same across all branches of the military during World War II. The contents of each file will vary based on the circumstances of the MIA status or death. Using these documents you can learn a lot about your service member's history, and often piece together some of his training history.

Report of Burial

A Report of Burial contained the soldier's name, date of death, place of death, and a copy of his identification tag, if located, stamped onto the form using an addressograph machine. The report also contained the grave location of the soldier with the names of the men buried on either side of him, to help with identification purposes. At the time the report was created, if the emergency contact and religious information was available, it was also added. A list of personal effects was included if any were found on the body. Personal effects for the soldier not located on his person at death or recovery were inventoried separately.

A Report of Burial will be in a file created during the war by the AGRS. You may not encounter this form in every IDPF. If the soldier was recovered after the war, it is possible the AGRS or other unit used a Report of Interment.

Report of Interment

The Report of Interment was used for several reasons by the AGRS. The report was used when remains of an unknown solider were disinterred after the war ended to attempt identification. It was also used when the AGRS disinterred soldiers to move them to a permanent cemetery from a temporary cemetery and when laying out a permanent cemetery.

If Deceased was Unidentified

If the deceased was unable to be identified, a form which allowed for fingerprinting was used and inserted into the file. This form contained space to list a physical description and information on personal effects or other things which might help identify the deceased.

The next step in attempting to identify a soldier was contacting St. Louis or Washington, D.C. to obtain the dental records and fingerprints for soldiers who may be the unidentified soldier. Lists of soldiers who were MIA and unrecovered in the location of the unidentified soldier were compiled based on battle maps and plans. The units that had been in the area were narrowed down and those who were still unaccounted for would have records requested.

In some cases, when the information was received by the AGRS, it would contain basic training information with locations and dates as detailed. More extensive details from a service file are usually not found in the IDPF. Pages from the IDPF may be found within a service file.

Casualty Report

The Battle Casualty Report (Army and Army Air Forces) or the Casualty Report (Navy and Marine Corps) had the usual service information in addition to the date of casualty, which could have been designated as MIA or KIA, name of the next of kin and relationship to the deceased as well as the date notified of the casualty.

Report of Death

The Report of Death listed the deceased's usual information, branch of service, date of birth and death, date of active entry in service, where he was killed, emergency contact and beneficiary information. There was a section at the bottom of the form which allowed for additional information about the deceased. Usually some statement about when the evidence of death was received by the war department was included in this section.

Telegrams

Telegrams or letters sent to the next-of-kin regarding MIA and KIA statuses may be found within the IDPF.

Inventory of Effects

The Inventory of Effects form described the items collected to be sent to the family. It was broken out by package number in case there were multiple packages to send to a next of kin. These were accompanied by a letter to the family regarding the remains. There was a duplicate letter sent which had to be signed by the next of kin acknowledging the receipt of effects. In the case of officers, there may have been multiple Inventory of Effect forms created from the officer's remains and his personal belongings in camp or held somewhere other than where he died.

Prisoner of War Cards or Information

If a soldier was taken as a German POW, their IDPF may contain the POW cards and information from captured German records or the Red Cross. These cards may include photos of the soldier. Those taken as a POW by the Japanese often do not have the card in their IDPF.

Report of Investigation Area Search

Searches for soldiers who were MIA or buried in isolated graves were conducted after the war ended. AGRS visited locations provided by units who had provided coordinates or locations of isolated graves. GRS also visited towns near battles and known plane crash sites to interview town and church officials and the townspeople regarding isolated graves. Included with this report are often pages from the Missing Air Crew Report (MACR). The MACR will be explained in the chapter on Records Created in the Field.

Checklist of Unknowns

Included with the Report of Investigation Area Search, if remains were recovered, is the Checklist of Unknowns. When a soldier was recovered from an isolated grave, he was given an X-number in place of a service number. All identifying information obtainable at that moment was documented, and the remains, plus any personal effects, were transported to a temporary cemetery. At the cemetery, an attempt at identification would be made. If this was accomplished, the X-file documentation was incorporated into the IDPF for the identified soldier.

Often included with these reports are testimony from officials and townspeople, maps, a Notice of Disinterment, and additional details about the Soldier Dead.

Disinterment Directive

The Disinterment Directive form contained the basic identifying information on the Soldier Dead: Name, rank, service number, date of death, cemetery name and location of grave, name and address of next of kin, condition of remains, date disinterred, and remains prepared.

Receipt of Remains

The form was used for repatriated remains, not buried in overseas cemeteries. This form was signed by the next of kin or funeral home receiving the remains when they arrived in the hometown.

Family Correspondence

IDPFs often contain correspondence from family members asking about personal effects, the circumstances of their soldier's death, or location and repatriation of the remains. The correspondence can be heartbreaking or graphic, depending on the nature of the letter.

Records Created by the Graves Registration Service

The GRS created records which were occasionally included in a soldier's IDPF. These included the following forms.[31]

Collecting Point Register

The Collecting Point Register was created at a collection site, and was not a standard form. It included name, rank, serial number, evacuation number and other pieces of information relevant to the death and location of the remains.

Certificate of Identity

The Certificate of Identity was Form DD 565, which was signed by the person identifying the remains in the field. It may have been a comrade in arms, or anyone who could present evidence as to the identity of the Soldier Dead.

Report of Recovery of Unknown

The Report of Recovery of Unknown contained information regarding the unknown Soldier Dead, where he was recovered, the condition of the remains, and anything that might identify him in the future.

Grave Plot Chart

The Grave Plot Chart was a standard form DD 568, created for every plot in a cemetery. Names and grave numbers of all deceased were listed here.

Historical File

The file was a register of interments and additional records held by the GRS to identify both cemetery burials and isolated burials.

Burial Overseas

Each temporary cemetery had different policies, but ceremonies were held to honor the dead daily, or as often as a military chaplain could be spared. In Margraten, Holland, burial services were held daily by the military chaplain sent from headquarters. The company of GRS men at Margraten performed their own small ceremony with the village priest after the official one to honor the dead they had buried that day. Upon conclusion of the ceremony, a firing squad shot their volleys, Taps was played and the flag was lowered from the flag pole with great reverence.[32]

Notification of Family

The family was notified of MIA and KIA statuses usually within a couple of weeks to months of the event by the War Department. The War Department then published lists of the Missing, Dead, or Prisoners of War (POW) service members and their next of kin in the newspapers. Usually the next of kin's address was included in these lists. These notices appeared as soon as a few weeks after the status changes, but could take three months or more before the names would appear in the paper.

What was not usually explained to the family was exactly how their soldier died. They were not told about the condition of the body at death or upon locating the remains. The family was not told if there were personal effects on the body. This made it difficult for the family who was grieving for their soldier and could not understand why no effects were coming back.

Final Disposition of Remains after the War

After the war ended, the U.S. government began working with overseas officials to secure the authorization to use ports, disinter remains in private cemeteries, and authorization to use rail and waterways to transport remains to major sea ports.[33] Once this was in place, the government was able to contact families of the dead to inquire about their wishes for the final burial.

There were four major areas of concentration during the repatriation process. These were: to locate isolated graves and identify the remains buried within these graves, condense the cemeteries into as few as possible across Europe and Asia, and return our honored dead to the U.S., if requested by the family.[34]

AGRS went in search of unfound remains and began disinterring remains from temporary cemeteries in enemy lands. Every effort was made to find all MIA and those killed in action.

The government began notifying families of the location of temporary burial beginning in late 1946, and continued for several years afterward. Depending on when the soldier died, it is possible he had been buried overseas two or more years before the family was notified of the location.

The AGRS men stationed overseas after the war ended had the duty to now disinter and prepare our country's honored dead for final burial at home or overseas. Civilians in the areas where the temporary cemeteries had been built were hired to help with disinterment. What they uncovered were remains in all states of decomposition. Disinfectants were used to help mask the odor, but did little good.

The AGRS procedure was to take disinterred remains to the morgue where "all clothing and flesh were removed, then burned" before the remaining skeleton was cleaned and sterilized for final placement in the hermetically sealed casket.35 During the entire disinterment process, identities were checked, double checked, and triple checked before they were finally laid to rest in their caskets and boxed for shipping. It was a job few would want to do, but the AGRS men carried it out with great dignity and decorum for the soldiers who gave the ultimate sacrifice.

The Decision of Final Burial

In 1947, the government gave families several options for final burial. The most commonly selected options were numbers 1 and 2.

1. The option to have the remains disinterred, at government expense, and returned to a U.S. National Cemetery for burial. If a family chose to have the remains buried in a non-National Cemetery, the cost would fall to the family. In many cases,

the families could not afford the expense and had to leave their family member buried overseas.

2. The other option was reburial in a permanent American cemetery overseas.

In rare cases, remains were allowed to remain in civilian cemeteries where they would be cared for.

I have seen a file in which the soldier was of Italian-American descent. His parents asked that his remains be sent to Italy to be buried in the hometown of his parents, rather than an overseas American Cemetery or repatriated.

The disinterment and repatriation process took several years after the war ended, partly due to a shortage of materials for cases for the caskets, and a shortage of metal for the caskets themselves. One of the first shipments to Europe took place in May 1947, when the Liberty Ship Joseph V. Connolly was sent to deliver steel coffins. The coffins were "made of steel with bronze finish" and "were seamless, a cover set on a rubber gasket is sealed with thirty-two lugs."[36] These coffins were placed into a wooden shipping case after the Soldier Dead was placed inside and the lid sealed. The shipping cases had the name, rank, and serial number of the soldier inscribed on the case. The shipping cases were stored in warehouses, when possible, or stacked in fields and covered with tarps until they were ready for transport by rail or water to the ports. Upon transport to the ports, each shipping case was covered with an American Flag. The flag remained on the case until it was delivered to a home or funeral home in the U.S.

Once the Soldier Dead were returned to the U.S., they were sent to one of fifty receiving stations set up in to receive the casketed remains. The caskets were transported to these receiving stations on converted Army and Navy train cars which held 66 shipping cases per car. Each funeral train held an honor guard which traveled with the boxed caskets.[37]

The soldiers who remained behind at the request of their families, or who were Unknowns, were interred in a permanent American Military Cemetery, which became part of the American Battle Monuments Commission. Many airmen or tankers whose remains could not be distinguished from one another, were given group burials in the U.S., often at Jefferson Barracks or Arlington National Cemetery. For those who remained, burial services were held for each Soldier Dead at the permanent cemetery. Burial flags were then sent to the next-of-kin.

It is a common misconception that the government paid for every penny spent to repatriate the remains of a service member after World War II. The government paid for the return of remains to the U.S. and covered the burial in National Veterans Cemeteries. Those families who did not wish to have their soldier buried in a National Cemetery had to pay for private burial. There are many families who could not afford to bury their family member, and their only option was to leave them buried overseas.

I've heard many say there is no other honored burial place that exists for our service members who died in World War II than our ABMC cemeteries. Thousands of families, who chose to repatriate their family members, will disagree with that comment. Some have vehemently stated money was never an option in making this decision. There is evidence in many IDPFs that money was a huge factor in making the decision.

The decisions made during and after World War II should be viewed through the historical lens, which means those decisions are not ours to judge. Few living today were the ones faced with making the decisions required after someone died.

Why did families choose to leave their service member overseas?

Many factors entered the decision for final burial. A few reasons included in IDPFs include:

- Money

- The wishes of the service member who, if he died, wished to be buried with his buddies.

- Wishes of the family to leave their service member with his buddies.

- Family grief.

- Easier for the widow or parents not to have the remains.

Standing in an ABMC cemetery, we marvel at the beauty and serenity it brings. We can say in that moment that the right decision was made leaving the service member here. However, on some level, that makes the decisions of those who brought their service member home, wrong.

Nothing that happened in World War II or after, is ours to judge. We were not there having the experience or making the decisions. The families chose what was best for them at the time, while dealing with tremendous grief most of us cannot imagine.

As you continue to move through your World War II research, I encourage you to view it through the historical lens without judgment. Perhaps even try putting yourself in the shoes of those making decisions if you do find judgment creeping in.

Identification and Repatriation of World War II MIAs Today

The Defense Prisoners of War Missing Personnel Office (DPAA) is currently responsible for recovering and identifying remains from World War II to Vietnam. Currently the process to identify remains and create casualty profiles of missing personnel is lengthy. It is not just a matter of obtaining a next-of-kin's DNA and testing. A lot of research goes into the battles and areas where soldiers fell or were buried to narrow down a list of possible unresolved casualties. Many military records are consulted to gleam any additional clues to help identify recovered remains.

The U.S. government needs your help if you have a family member who was MIA or unrecoverable during any war. You can help by submitting DNA samples for use in identification efforts as remains are recovered. To learn more, visit DPAA's website at http://www.dpaa.mil/Our-Missing/World-War-II/

Finding the Answers

The answers to many of these questions were contained in this short history of the AGRS and IDPF documents. Would you like to learn more about these files, how to navigate them, view their contents, and better understand the information they contain? Would you like to learn more about the family stories that can be told from this file?

If the answer is YES, you might be interested in our course, Finding the Answers in the IDPF on our site WWII Education (http://wwi-ieducation.com). You can find it listed in the Store.

Researching your service member's history can be complex. The World War II Research and Writing Center provides research experts to tackle your most challenging research questions. Contact us at info@wwiirwc.com for project details and costs. We have researchers on-site at the National Archives facilities to obtain materials within a few weeks, and a network of researchers and tour guides around the globe.

General Questions

Who created these files? Do I need to explore the history of the Graves Registration Unit who recovered my soldier?

When were families notified about the MIA status or confirmed death?

What did the government tell (or not tell) the families through official correspondence when they were notified about the death?

What happened to the remains that were identified or not identified?

What did the government pay for as part of final burial?

Why did some families choose to leave their service member buried overseas? Was money ever an issue?

Family Questions

What are the death details? When, where, how, did he suffer?

Where is he buried?

He died as a POW. When can I have his body back?

What happened to the personal effects? Why are some missing?

Who receives his death benefits and insurance?

Who determines where the remains are to be permanently interred? What happens if the widow of the serviceman remarried after his death and prior to the final decisions?

What personal effects were recovered and sent home? For example, why did one soldier have a $200,000 personal check in his personal effects overseas?

What happens if he is never recovered and remains in MIA status?

What happened to the cemeteries in which our honored dead rest?

What family history information and family dynamics do we see in these files?

What family secrets and drama are uncovered?

General Biographical and Service History Questions

The following questions are often asked by family members re-searching their service member, but also European grave adopters who honor the memory of our American service members. European grave adopters generally want to know the basics of the individual's death and to locate family, and a photograph. On the other side of that coin, there are some grave adopters who want to know the individual's entire service history, locate family, and photographs. These are some questions which are asked.

When was service member born?

When did he enlist, or what was the induction date?

What was his service number?

What was his training like? Where, when, what did he learn?

If applicable, when did he become an officer?

What unit(s) was he in?

Who was his next-of-kin? Is there any evidence of a remarriage of the widow?

Are there any living family members with whom I can talk to?

Are there any surviving photographs?

Is there information about other relatives in service?

When was he KIA, declared MIA or POW, or had a FOD? What were the circumstances surrounding his death and recovery?

When and where was he buried?

Selected Resources

American Battle Monuments Commission.
http://www.abmc.gov

American Battle Monuments Commission Archives. Luxembourg City, Luxembourg. Air Force Accident Reports. Aviation Archaeology.com.

Army Mortuary Affairs History Page.
http://www.qmmuseum.lee.army.mil/main.html?n=1

Department of the Army. Field Manual 10-63 Graves Registration. Washington, D.C.: United States Government Printing Office, 1952.

Department of the Army. Field Manual 10-29 Quartermaster Graves Registration Company. Washington, D.C.: United States Government Printing Office, 1952.

Department of the Army. Technical Manual 10-240 Deceased Personnel in the United States, Excluding Alaska. Washington, D.C.: United States Government Printing Office, 1947.

Department of the Army. Technical Manual 10-285 Deceased Personnel. Washington, D.C.: United States Government Printing Office, 1947.

Department of the Army. Technical Manual 10-285 Deceased Personnel. Washington, D.C.: United States Government Printing Office, 1947.

Department of the Navy. Disposition of Navy, Marine Corps and Coast Guard World War II Dead. Washington D.C.: Navy Department, undated.

Individual Deceased Personnel Files. National Personnel Records Center, St. Louis, MO.

Official Military Personnel Files. National Personnel Records Center, St. Louis, MO.

Office of the Quartermaster General. History of the American Graves Registration Service. Q.M.C. in Europe Volume I to September 1920,

Volume II, and Volume III. Consolidated reprint of Volumes I, II, and III. Undated.

Shomon, Joseph James. Crosses in the Wind. New York: Stratford House, Inc., 1947.

Sledge, Michael. Soldier Dead. How We Recover, Identify, Bury, and Honor Our Military Fallen. New York: Columbia University Press, 2005.

World War II Education

http://wwiieducation.com

World War II Research and Writing Center

http://wwiirwc.com

WW2 US Medical Research Centre

https://www.med-dept.com/

Notes

1 Shomon, Joseph James. Crosses in the Wind,(Netherlands: Keulers, Geleen: 1947, 1991), 160.

2 History, website American Battle Monuments Commission, (http:// abmc.gov/commission/history.php 6 September 2013).

3 Richardson, Eudora Ramsay, and Allan, Sherman, Quartermaster Supply in the European Theater of Operations in World War II Volume VII Graves Registration. (Camp Lee, VA: The Quartermaster School, 1948), 1.

4 Richardson, Eudora Ramsay, and Allan, Sherman, Quartermaster Supply in the European Theater of Operations in World War II Volume VII Graves Registration. (Camp Lee, VA: The Quartermaster School, 1948), 1.

5 Richardson, Eudora Ramsay, and Allan, Sherman, Quartermaster Supply in the European Theater of Operations in World War II Volume VII Graves Registration. (Camp Lee, VA: The Quartermaster School, 1948), 1.

6 Department of the Army. Field Manual 10-29 Quartermaster Graves Registration Company. (Washington, D.C.: United States Government Printing Office, 1952), 30-31.

7 Department of the Army. Field Manual 10-29 Quartermaster Graves Registration Company. (Washington, D.C.: United States Government Printing Office, 1952), 31.

8 Department of the Army. Field Manual 10-29 Quartermaster Graves Registration Company. (Washington, D.C.: United States Government Printing Office, 1952), 31-32.

9 Department of the Army. Field Manual 10-29 Quartermaster Graves Registration Company. (Washington, D.C.: United States Government Printing Office, 1952), 32.

10 Department of the Army. Field Manual 10-29 Quartermaster Graves Registration Company. (Washington, D.C.: United States Government Printing Office, 1952), 27-28.

11 Department of the Army. Field Manual 10-29 Quartermaster Graves Registration Company. (Washington, D.C.: United States Government Printing Office, 1952), 29-30.

12 Department of the Army. Field Manual 10-29 Quartermaster Graves Registration Company. (Washington, D.C.: United States Government Printing Office, 1952), 30.

13 Department of the Army. Field Manual 10-29 Quartermaster Graves Registration Company. (Washington, D.C.: United States Government Printing Office, 1952), 30.

14 Department of the Army. Field Manual 10-29 Quartermaster Graves Registration Company. (Washington, D.C.: United States Government Printing Office, 1952), 36.

15 Department of the Army. Field Manual 10-29 Quartermaster Graves Registration Company. (Washington, D.C.: United States Government Printing Office, 1952), 37.

16 Department of the Army. Field Manual 10-29 Quartermaster Graves Registration Company. (Washington, D.C.: United States Government Printing Office, 1952), 37.

17 Department of the Army. Field Manual 10-29 Quartermaster Graves Registration Company. (Washington, D.C.: United States Government Printing Office, 1952), 37-38.

18 Department of the Army. Field Manual 10-29 Quartermaster Graves Registration Company. (Washington, D.C.: United States Government Printing Office, 1952), 38.

19 Crosses at Normandy, Jun 1944, digital story, U.S. Army Quartermaster Foundation (http://www.qmfound.com/crosses.htm 6 September 2013); citing story of Colonel Elbert E. Legg.

20 Crosses at Normandy, Jun 1944, digital story, U.S. Army Quartermaster Foundation (http://www.qmfound.com/crosses.htm 6 September 2013); citing story of Colonel Elbert E. Legg.

21 Department of the Army. Field Manual 10-63 Graves Registration. (Washington, D.C.: United States Government Printing Office, 1945), 16-18.

22 Department of the Army. Field Manual 10-63 Graves Registration. (Washington, D.C.: United States Government Printing Office, 1945), 16-18.

23 Shomon, Joseph James. Crosses in the Wind,(Netherlands: Keulers, Geleen: 1947, 1991), 91.

24 Shomon, Joseph James. Crosses in the Wind,(Netherlands: Keulers, Geleen: 1947, 1991), 137-138.

25 Shomon, Joseph James. Crosses in the Wind,(Netherlands: Keulers, Geleen: 1947, 1991), 15.

26 Department of the Army. Field Manual 10-63 Graves Registration. (Washington, D.C.: United States Government Printing Office, 1945), 23-24.

27 Division of the Federal Register, the National Archives. Code of Federal Regulations of the United States of America. 1946 Supplement. Washington, D.C.:U.S. Government Printing Office, 1947, 5826.

28 Service Record of 1st Lt. Robert E. Bishop, serial no. 0210591, letter to the Secretary of Navy dated 17 Jan 1945. NPRC, St. Louis, Missouri.

29 Service Record of 1st Lt. Robert E. Bishop, serial no. 0210591, letter to the Robert Bishop's parents dated 22 Jan 1946. NPRC, St. Louis, Missouri.

30 Individual Deceased Personnel File, Samuel W. Crowder, service no. 2868801; Board Proceedings Number 1961, Proceedings of Board of Review dated 25 April 1949, p.7.

31 Department of the Army. Field Manual 10-29 Quartermaster Graves Registration Company. (Washington, D.C.: United States Government Printing Office, 1952), 52-53.

32 Shomon, Joseph James. Crosses in the Wind,(Netherlands: Keulers, Geleen: 1947, 1991), 66-67.

33 Richardson, Eudora Ramsay, and Allan, Sherman, Quartermaster Supply in the European Theater of Operations in World War II Volume VII Graves Registration. (Camp Lee, VA: The Quartermaster School, 1948), 87.

34 Richardson, Eudora Ramsay, and Allan, Sherman, Quartermaster Supply in the European Theater of Operations in World War II Volume VII Graves Registration. (Camp Lee, VA: The Quartermaster School, 1948), 88.

35 Shomon, Joseph James. Crosses in the Wind,(Netherlands: Keulers, Geleen: 1947, 1991), 147.

36 WAR-DEAD COFFINS ON WAY TO EUROPE. 1947. New York Times (1923-Current file), May 15, 1947. http://search.proquest.com/docview/107912796 by?accountid=38403 (accessed August 27, 2013).

37 WAR-DEAD COFFINS ON WAY TO EUROPE. 1947. New York Times (1923-Current file), May 15, 1947. http://search.proquest.com/docview/107912796 by?accountid=38403 (accessed August 27, 2013).